S0-AGK-271

Protecting the EARTH'S ANIMALS

Saving Marine Mammals

Whales, Dolphins, Seals, and More

DIANE BAILEY

Protecting the Earth's Animals

Animal Testing:
Attacking a Controversial Problem

Battling Wildlife Poachers:
The Fight to Save Elephants, Rhinos, Lions, Tigers, and More

Dogs and Cats:
Saving Our Precious Pets

Pollination Problems:
The Battle to Save Bees and Other Vital Animals

Rescuing Primates:
Gorillas, Chimps, and Monkeys

Saving Marine Mammals:
Whales, Dolphins, Seals, and More

Saving Ocean Animals:
Sharks, Turtles, Coral, and Fish

Saving the Rainforests:
Inside the World's Most Diverse Habitat

Saving Marine Mammals

Whales, Dolphins, Seals, and More

BY DIANE BAILEY

Mason Crest

450 Parkway Drive, Suite D
Broomall, PA 19008
www.masoncrest.com

© 2018 by Mason Crest, an imprint of National Highlights, Inc.

All rights reserved. No part of this publication may be reproduced or transmitted in any form or by any means, electronic or mechanical, including photocopying, recording, taping, or any information storage and retrieval system, without permission from the publisher.

Printed and bound in the United States of America.

Series ISBN: 978-1-4222-3872-1
Hardback ISBN: 978-1-4222-3878-3
EBook ISBN: 978-1-4222-7915-1

First printing
1 3 5 7 9 8 6 4 2

Produced by Shoreline Publishing Group LLC
Santa Barbara, California
Editorial Director: James Buckley Jr.
Designer: Patty Kelley
www.shorelinepublishing.com

Library of Congress Cataloging-in-Publication Data
Names: Bailey, Diane, 1966- author.
Title: Saving marine mammals : whales, dolphins, seals, and more / by Diane Bailey.
Description: Broomall, PA : Mason Crest, [2017] |
Series: Protecting the Earth's animals | Includes bibliographical references and index.
Identifiers: LCCN 2017001351| ISBN 9781422238783 (hardback) | ISBN 9781422238721 (series) |
    ISBN 9781422279151 (ebook)
Subjects: LCSH: Marine mammals–Conservation–Juvenile literature. | Wildlife conservation–Juvenile
    literature.
Classification: LCC QL713.2 .B35 2017 | DDC 333.95/9–dc23 LC record available at https://lccn.loc.
    gov/2017001351

Cover photographs by Dreamstime.com: Andrew Astbury (seal); Tom Dowd (dolphin);
Paul Wolf (whale).

QR Codes disclaimer:

You may gain access to certain third party content ("Third-Party Sites") by scanning and using the QR Codes that appear in this publication (the "QR Codes"). We do not operate or control in any respect any information, products, or services on such Third-Party Sites linked to by us via the QR Codes included in this publication, and we assume no responsibility for any materials you may access using the QR Codes. Your use of the QR Codes may be subject to terms, limitations, or restrictions set forth in the applicable terms of use or otherwise established by the owners of the Third-Party Sites. Our linking to such Third-Party Sites via the QR Codes does not imply an endorsement or sponsorship of such Third-Party Sites, or the information, products, or services offered on or through the Third- Party Sites, nor does it imply an endorsement or sponsorship of this publication by the owners of such Third-Party Sites.

CONTENTS

KEY ICONS TO LOOK FOR

Words to Understand: These words with their easy-to-understand definitions will increase the reader's understanding of the text, while building vocabulary skills.

Sidebars: This boxed material within the main text allows readers to build knowledge, gain insights, explore possibilities, and broaden their perspectives by weaving together additional information to provide realistic and holistic perspectives.

Educational Videos: Readers can view videos by scanning our QR codes, providing them with additional educational content to supplement the text. Examples include news coverage, moments in history, speeches, iconic moments, and much more!

Text-Dependent Questions: These questions send the reader back to the text for more careful attention to the evidence presented here.

Research Projects: Readers are pointed toward areas of further inquiry connected to each chapter. Suggestions are provided for projects that encourage deeper research and analysis.

Series Glossary of Key Terms: This back-of-the-book glossary contains terminology used throughout this series. Words found here increase the reader's ability to read and comprehend higher-level books and articles in this field.

INTRODUCTION

A small plane criss-crossed the ocean off the coasts of Florida and Georgia. Twenty-five miles out to sea, right turn, 25 miles back, left turn, 25 miles out to sea, right turn . . .

The plane's crew was looking for North Atlantic right whales. These whales are a critically endangered species, with only about 550 left. They are slow swimmers, and they tend to stay near the surface, which makes them much more likely to get in the way of boat traffic. If the plane's crew spotted any whales, they would warn nearby boats to steer clear.

After a few hours, the crew had not seen any whales and was ready to head in. Then a splash in the water got their attention. When they looked closer, they recognized what had made it—a right whale named Punctuation. Next to her was her newborn calf. After giving birth in the warm southern waters, Punctuation was heading back north with her calf to cooler water.

The two whales didn't make it. Three months later, in May, the story took a tragic turn. A young right whale was found dead in the water near Massachusetts. Scientists

Small boats are used to safely approach whales.

recognized it as Punctuation's calf. They examined the body and found the calf had several broken bones as well as slashes on its body from ship propellers.

The area where Punctuation's calf died has heavy shipping traffic. Even though large ships are required to travel slowly—less than 10 knots (11 mph/18 kph)—it's still very risky for the whales.

It was a terrible loss, especially since North Atlantic right whales only give birth once every three to five years. The species was hunted close to extinction by the 1930s. Even though they have now been protected for close to 80 years, they have not rebounded.

Although there are similar stories of marine mammals in trouble all over the world, there is good news, too. There are just as many stories of the ways people are helping them.

WORDS TO UNDERSTAND

circulatory relating to how blood moves around in the body

echolocation a way that animals can use sound echoes to find objects

ecosystem the places that species live, and how they interact with each other and their environment

keystone a part of a system that everything else depends on

pelt the outer skin and fur of a mammal

AT HOME IN THE WATER

Whales killed in traffic accidents. Dolphins with measles. Starving sea lions and overheated polar bears. All over the world, marine mammals are facing problems. Some species have become extinct. They are threatened by everything from hunting and fishing to ship strikes, pollution, and global warming. But there are also some success stories as people learn more about marine mammals and how to protect them.

Sentries of the Sea

Millions of different species live in the ocean, but only a tiny fraction are mammals. There are only about 125 different species of marine mammals in the world, which makes their survival very important. Marine mammals play a key part in keeping **ecosystems** healthy. For one thing, they are larger than most other marine species, so they eat more. This helps keep the populations of smaller animals,

Life of a marine mammal.

such as fish, shrimp, and squid under control. Mammals can also be hosts for other types of life. Barnacles, for example, are small creatures that attach themselves to the bodies of gray whales. That way, they get a free ride to better ocean-feeding grounds. The health of marine mammals says a lot about ocean life in general—if they are doing well, then it's a good bet other marine life is too.

Marine mammals fall into four main categories. Cetaceans are the main swimmers and include whales, dolphins, and porpoises. Pinnipeds are another major group that includes seals, sea lions, and walruses. (Seals and sea lions are similar, but sea lions are better adapted for moving around on land.) Manatees and dugongs belong to the sirenia category. They are commonly known as "sea cows," which is a perfect description for these large, slow-moving animals. Sea otters and polar bears are in the category of marine fissipeds. They have feet and are related to land animals. However, they are still categorized as marine mammals because they depend on the sea to survive.

All mammals, whether they live on land or in the sea, share some characteristics. They give birth to live babies who drink milk from their mothers when they are very young. They breathe using lungs, and have some kind of hair or fur. They are warm-blooded, meaning that their body temperature stays the same even when the air or water around them gets very hot or cold. That's one reason marine mammals can get so big—they need a lot of fat to stay warm in the water.

Seals have thick coats of fat to help them survive the cold water.

Ocean Evolution

About 50 million years ago, things on land were getting tough. Mammals had evolved from amphibians and reptiles and their populations on land were growing larger and stronger. As they did, the competition for food and resources got more intense.

The situation was different in the ocean. At that time, the oceans were becoming easier to get to as the continents slowly drifted apart. That created large areas of open water and more coastline. The ocean was also packed with fish and other creatures, making it a great source of food. Land-based mammals just had to "figure out" how to take advantage of it. Gradually, some land mammals began to adapt to living in water, and they evolved into the marine mammals seen today.

Marine mammals have certain characteristics that make them ideal for living

Coral reefs are made from animal skeletons.

DON'T LOSE THE KEYS!

For marine life, an underwater kelp forest is like a grocery store and apartment building rolled into one. Lots of different kinds of fish live there. Gray whales use the long, wavy stalks to hide from killer whales, while birds take shelter from storms. While many species live or feed among the kelp, there are some that just like to snack on the kelp itself. Sea urchins are particularly hungry creatures and can devour a kelp forest. That's where sea otters come in; they find kelp-dwelling sea urchins quite tasty. That keeps the population of urchins in check, which preserves the kelp forests. Because of their job munching on urchins, sea otters are considered a **keystone** species. Without them, there would be a drastic change in how the ecosystem worked.

in the ocean. One is the shape of their bodies, which are streamlined to make them better swimmers. Humans have arms and legs and ears and noses sticking out all over. Whales and dolphins, on the other hand, are shaped more

ARE YOU SMARTER THAN A WHALE?

That depends on whom you ask. (The whale might say no!) We humans usually consider ourselves the most intelligent creatures on the planet, but that may be because we don't understand other animals. Scientists now know that whales and dolphins are very intelligent and social, just like people. Some of them call cetaceans "non-human" people, and think they should be treated as equal to humans. At a conference in 2010, several experts drew up a declaration of "cetacean rights." It said that dolphins and whales should be recognized as individuals and free to move around as they pleased. The movement is catching on. In 2013, the government of India made it illegal to hold dolphins, whales, and porpoises in captivity. If we need to solve the world's problems, we might want to save the marine mammals. Once we figure out how to listen, they might have the answers!

like bottles. What once were legs turned into flippers and fins. Their ears got much smaller (but they actually still have great hearing).

The insides of marine mammal bodies also went through a lot of changes. Their blood and organs can hold a lot of oxygen. Marine mammals can stay underwater for several minutes, and sometimes more than an hour! It's important to stay warm in cold ocean water, so the **circulatory** system in a marine mammal is

Sea otters have thick fur that keeps them warm even when wet.

designed to transfer heat throughout their bodies. They also have thick layers of fat. Polar bears and sea otters use their fur to stay warm. Even when their fur is wet, it traps a layer of warm air next to their bodies.

It can be difficult to see through murky water. Sound is a more dependable sense. Water is denser than air, which lets it carry sound waves much farther. Whales and dolphins use **echolocation** to help them perceive things underwater. They send out sound signals that bounce off objects and come back to them. It's like a sound boomerang! Based on what these echoes sound like and how long it takes them to come back, the return sounds tell them things like how large an object is, and how far away it is. Cetaceans also use a large vocabulary of clicks, whistles, and rumbling sounds to communicate with each other. Some of the noises are very loud—louder than a jet engine or a rock concert, and can be heard for hundreds of miles.

Whale mothers use sound to communicate with their young.

Centuries of Change

During the process of evolution, animal species sometimes become extinct. Those that cannot adapt to a changing environment, don't survive. Usually, extinction is a very gradual process. As one species dies off, another takes its place. It happens over millions of years. On rare occasions, there is a mass extinction. A huge event changes the environment dramatically. It happens so fast that many species die within a short time. This happened 65 million years ago, when a meteor hit the Earth. It caused a mass extinction of dinosaurs.

The rise of humans is not exactly a meteor. It may feel that way to wildlife, though. In the 1700s and 1800s, for example, there was a huge demand for seals and whales. Seals were valuable for their **pelts**, which were used to made fur coats. Whales had lots of blubber (fat) that could be turned into oil for light and heating.

Hunters started going after these animals aggressively well into the 20th century. Soon many populations were drastically reduced. Some went extinct or came close. After being hunted for decades, the Caribbean monk seal was officially declared extinct in 2008. The announcement came a little late—the seal had not been seen since the 1950s.

Human inventions have also made life harder for marine mammals. Electricity and gasoline motors certainly make travel easier for people, but those innovations turned out to be bad news for marine mammals. For example, as ship traffic increased on the Yangtze River in China, the Yangtze River dolphin could not compete. Scientists think the ships made so much noise that the dolphins could not hear well enough to find food. The dolphin became functionally extinct about 2007. That means that there could still be a few surviving individuals, but there are not enough for the species to come back.

There are some bright spots. The enormous northern elephant seal was once hunted for its blubber. By the late 1800s, it was thought to be extinct. However, a small population, less than 100 individuals, was discovered and protected. Slowly the elephant seals began to come back. Now, it's estimated there are about 150,000.

Another success story is the gray whale, which was hunted down to very low numbers by the 1940s. The gray whale became a protected species just in time. One group of gray whales, the western gray whale, is still endangered. The eastern gray whale has rebounded to about 20,000 individuals, probably close to the number before it was hunted.

One blue whale dives (rear) while another surfaces to breathe.

Turning the Tide

The blue whale is the largest animal on Earth. In fact, as far as scientists know, it is the biggest animal ever to live on Earth. Its stats are mind-boggling. A blue whale is 80-100 feet (24-30 m) long, and weighs 200 tons (181 metric tons). Its heart can weigh as much as a small car, and an elephant could stand on its tongue. (Don't worry, though, the whale won't swallow the elephant—blue whales prefer to eat krill, which are like tiny shrimp.)

Even smaller marine mammals can be pretty big. Walruses and elephant seals are huge. Polar bears can weigh several hundred pounds. Unfortunately, size has some disadvantages. Bigger animals are more likely to go extinct. They need much larger habitats to live in, and they are slower to respond to changes in the environment. This makes them more vulnerable.

Larger mammals also tend to have fewer babies, and less often. Some species give birth only once every few years. Even if only a few individuals die—especially females—it can have a devastating effect on the population as a whole.

There have been some positive steps to help marine mammals. Governments are stepping up to protect marine areas throughout the world. Hundreds of special-interest

Baby seals are very vulnerable to predators in the wild.

groups are focused on helping particular groups of animals, such as manatees or dolphins. There is much more awareness about environmental problems and how to fix them. But there is still a lot of work to be done.

 ## TEXT-DEPENDENT QUESTIONS

1. Give an example of an animal that is a pinniped.

2. Why do whales and dolphins use echolocation?

3. What caused the mass extinction of dinosaurs 65 million years ago?

 ## RESEARCH PROJECT

Choose a marine mammal that has become extinct, such as the Caribbean monk seal or the Yangtze River dolphin, and find out more about it. What was the situation like for this animal a century ago? What factors contributed to its extinction?

WORDS TO UNDERSTAND

activist someone who works for a particular cause or issue

biodiverse having a large variety of plants and animals in a particular area

by-catch fish or animals that are caught by accident as part of another catch

strand to get stuck and be unable to move

sustain to keep up something over a long period of time

FINDING A BALANCE

Humans are only one of the eight million species on the planet, but there are a lot of us. There are 7.4 billion people, according to the United Nations. All these people need food, and the ocean is one of the Earth's best food sources. People have always hunted and fished to feed themselves. As humans get hungrier, though, it also puts marine mammals at risk.

Save the Whales!

In the 1970s, as the environmental movement grew rapidly, "Save the Whales" was one of the most widely seen slogans. It started when people began to realize that the whales were dying out. The mighty blue whale was down to about only 5,000 individuals. That's about one whale per 28,000 square miles (72,000 sq km)—an area bigger than the whole state of West Virginia! Environmental groups started campaigns to educate people about how much whales were endangered. Some **activists** went out on boats and tried to stop whaling ships. Soon, people all over the world were concerned about whales.

Protests by people helped create laws to help whales.

By 1982, the International Whaling Commission (IWC) made a rule: no more commercial whaling, which means hunting whales for profit. It was a step in the right direction, but it has not solved the problem entirely. Although it is illegal to hunt whales commercially, it's still legal to kill some for scientific research. This is sometimes used as an excuse. Japanese hunters still capture whales in the name of science, even though they sell the meat. Iceland and Norway also have whaling operations.

News: Iceland whale hunting

Dolphins are also in danger from hunting. Hunting dolphins is traditional in some cultures. Taiji is a small town located on the east coast of Japan. Each year, the residents drive hundreds of dolphins into the bay, where they are killed and sold for food. In Peru, many thousands of dolphins are killed, even though it is illegal. People eat the dolphin meat and fishermen use it as bait to catch sharks. Marine mammals are not just killed for food. The fins of whales and dolphins are valued as trophies. Their teeth may be used in jewelry. Seals and otters are still hunted for their soft, warm fur.

It can be difficult to convince people to save a species,

but there is some success in the Solomon Islands, located about 500 miles (804 km) northeast of Australia. There, the residents on the island of Malaita have long killed dolphins for food and for their teeth. To help stop dolphin hunting there, a new program was started in 2015. An important part of the project is to encourage tourists to come to the area to watch dolphins swimming in their natural environment. That would help bring in money to the community without killing any dolphins.

Fishy Business

A small boat, a quiet lake, a bucket of bait: that might be what it's like for a weekend fisherman. It's much different for commercial fishermen. They sail out on huge fishing vessels with heavy equipment, often staying out for weeks at a time. They store the fish on ice until they come back to shore.

Finding fish is getting harder. Over the last decades, many species have been "overfished," which means that more fish are caught than can return the following year or season. That means fishermen are always looking for new places to find fish and to try more effective ways to catch them.

BATTLE ON THE HIGH SEAS

Sometimes, the rules just don't work. As long as they can get away with it, some fishermen and whalers will take whatever they can. Sure, it's illegal, but they have to get caught first. Catching them is exactly what the Sea Shepherd Conservation Society is trying to do. With a fleet of ships, the activists with Sea Shepherd keep track of animals that are in danger. Society members and boats have confronted several whaling ships

that illegally hunt whales in the Southern Ocean, next to Antarctica. The group uses some controversial methods, such as throwing stink bombs or ramming ships. The organization says these direct acts are necessary to make the illegal activities stop. However, they have also faced lawsuits for their actions, and some governments have told them to back off.

One way of catching fish is trawling. For this, a boat pulls a big net behind it in the water. Fish get trapped in the net. Dredging is a similar method. For that, a net is dragged along the bottom of the ocean. It can capture clams, scallops, and other animals that live on the ocean floor. Using nets is an easy way to catch fish, but the method can be very harmful to marine mammals. A net does not know the difference between a bluefin tuna and a bottlenose dolphin. A lot of extra **by-catch** ends up in the nets—that is, other fish and animals that the fishermen did not even want.

Blast fishing is a particularly harmful type of fishing. For

By-catch can be caught up in nets designed for food fish.

A beached whale is kept wet while a rescue is attempted.

this, fishermen throw dynamite into the water. When it explodes, it kills all the fish in the area. Some of them float to the surface, and the fishermen scoop them up. Blast fishing is cheap and easy, but it is deadly not only for fish, but for other animals as well. The loud explosions can damage the hearing of marine mammals, who depend on sound to navigate and communicate. It can also disorient them so they get lost. This can make them take a wrong turn and **strand** themselves on beaches or in shallow water, where they are stuck.

Governments all over the world have begun to recognize that commercial fishing causes terrible problems for

CASE STUDY: THE VANISHING VAQUITA

With dark patches around its eyes and thick black lips, the vaquita looks like it's wearing makeup. In fact, if you were to catch a glimpse of this little porpoise, you would probably think it was quite cute. Unfortunately, it's not very likely you will see one. For one thing, the vaquita is shy.

Try to snap a photo, and there's a good chance the vaquita will just disappear into the murky waters in the Gulf of California, off the west coast of Mexico. Another reason is even more discouraging: there are not very many vaquitas left to see. It is the single most endangered marine mammal in the world. As of 2016, marine biologists estimate there are only 57 individuals.

The main cause of death for the vaquita is getting caught in gillnets. These are like curtains of nets that hang in the water. Commercial fishermen use them to catch shrimp, as well as another endangered species, a type of fish called the totoaba. It lives in the same waters as the vaquita. The totoaba is worth a lot of money. A fish's swim bladder is a kind of balloon that helps it stay afloat. In parts of Asia, people think the totoaba's swim bladder is a good kind of medicine. One of them can sell for several thousand dollars. Killing the totoaba is illegal, but that doesn't stop some fishermen who want a quick payday. Unfortunately, when the totoaba get caught in nets, so do the vaquita. They die when they can't surface for air.

Even the loss of one vaquita per year is a lot for such a small population, but the numbers are even worse than that. From 2008 to 2015, the vaquita population shrank from 150 to only 60—more than 10 per year. At that point, the Mexican and U.S. governments stepped in. Working together, they have banned gillnet fishing in the Gulf of California. The Mexican navy is in charge of making sure fishermen don't break the law. It's a step in the right direction—now it's a question of seeing whether it will work.

mammal populations. Many have made laws about where it's okay to fish. They have made it illegal to fish in spots where marine mammals like to go. Fishermen have done their part, too. Many have redesigned nets and other equipment so they are less likely to trap by-catch. One strategy is to take advantage of marine mammals' strong sense of sound. Sometimes fishermen put "pingers" in their nets. These make sounds that scare away seals or dolphins. Some fishing boats send divers into the water to look for animals that can get caught in the nets and they can sometimes free them before they die.

Governments are battling against overfishing of key species.

In many places, there are also rules about how many fish can be taken over a certain period of time. Once the fishermen reach their limit, they have to stop. That way, an area is less likely to be overfished and there are enough fish left to **sustain** their populations.

Farming the Oceans

Doctors say that eating fish is good for humans. Many people in the world—especially in Asia—eat fish as a large part of their diet. There are a lot of people, though, and not as many fish in the sea as there used to be. For decades, populations of fish and shellfish have been dwindling. There's less cod, less salmon, less tuna. Meanwhile, the human population is growing—and so are their appetites.

This resulted in overfishing that has virtually wiped out some species. The ones that remain are getting harder to find. Humans can eat other things, of course, but marine mammals do not have a choice. They need to eat fish to survive. In the competition for food, they are losing to humans.

One alternative is aquaculture, which is like farming in water. "Fish farms" raise fish in pools of water on land,

Fish farms might be the answer to falling fish populations.

or in pens built in the ocean. The idea is to create a population that can sustain itself over time. There are some
disadvantages to fish farms. The fish farms in the ocean
are enclosed by nets. Seals and dolphins smell the fish,
swim over, and can get caught in the nets. If closed pens
are on land, solid walls are an alternative, with no nets for
mammals to get tangled in. And since they are completely
blocked off from the fish, they are less likely to get killed by
fishermen. When it's not possible to have a closed pen, one
solution is to put noisemaking devices on the nets to scare
away seals or other predators.

Fish farming is not a perfect solution. Farmed fish like

salmon, sea bass, and tuna are natural predators. Their diet consists of other fish farther down the food chain. That means farmers have to take several pounds of smaller, wild fish to make one pound of a big, farmed fish. The waste from these systems can also pollute the surrounding ecosystem. If fish farms are responsibly operated, however, they can provide a source of food for humans that has less impact on the other animals of the sea.

 ## TEXT-DEPENDENT QUESTIONS

1. Name one country that still hunts whales.

2. How can blast fishing harm marine mammals?

3. How are the U.S. and Mexican governments working to save the vaquita porpoise?

 ## RESEARCH PROJECT

Fish farming is a controversial topic. Do some research to make a list of the pros and cons, and then pick one of the downsides and think about a way to make it better.

WORDS TO UNDERSTAND

hypothermia a life-threatening condition of being too cold

sonar a human-made system that uses pulses of sound to locate underwater objects

toxin a poison

FOOTPRINTS IN THE SEA

It's easy to leave footprints in the sand. But footprints in the sea? Wouldn't they wash away instantly? For years, that's exactly what scientists thought. They believed the oceans were too big for humans to affect them. Now we know that is not true. The actions of humans have a tremendous impact on the ocean and the animals who live in it.

Climate Change

Melting ice in the Arctic and Antarctic. Rising sea levels. Violent storms and weird weather. These are all symptoms of climate change. For example, global warming is happening at the fastest pace since scientists began keeping records in 1880. Most scientists agree that people are to blame for global warming. Burning fossil fuels such as oil and coal produces a lot of carbon dioxide. In the atmosphere, the carbon dioxide acts as a trap. It keeps heat from the sun from escaping, which causes Earth to warm up.

Heat from factories contributes to rising temperatures.

Climate change causes many problems for wildlife. As ice melts in the Arctic and Antarctic, the water flows into the sea. Gradually, all that water is raising the sea levels and wiping out coastlines. Marine mammals that live in those areas are being forced out. Global warming is also making the water warmer, making it necessary for animals to move out of their traditional habitats.

Burning fossil fuels is a double-whammy for wildlife. Humans have become dependent on fossil fuels, and there is a lot of oil and gas in the Arctic. In the past, it wasn't worth it to try to drill for oil in the Arctic. It was too hard for ships and equipment to get through the ice. Now that the ice is

BACK FROM THE BRINK?

California sea lions can be heard on coast of central or northern California. They're loud! In the 1950s, there were only an estimated 10,000 California sea lions left. Since then, the population has expanded to about 300,000. Unfortunately, some of these

sea lions are in trouble again. In recent years, thousands of sea lions began staggering onto the coast. Biologists found that the sea lions were starving. Scientists think the water had gotten too warm for the fish that sea lions eat. By 2015, sea lions had another problem. Algae in the water produced a **toxin** when it bloomed. Fish ate the algae, and sea lions ate the poisoned fish. Scientists don't know what causes the toxic blooms. However, they have found that it is worse in warm water. Fortunately, hundreds of sea lions have been rescued and helped at the Marine Mammal Center in California. By studying what's happening to the rescued animals, scientists may be able to help solve their problems.

melting, it's gotten easier. Several countries, including the United States, are already drilling in the Arctic. That disturbs the habitats of animals living there. It also increases the risk for an oil spill in the water.

People are working to combat climate change. There are international agreements in place to cut down on the amount of fossil fuels used worldwide. Many companies and governments are working to find renewable sources of energy, such as wind and solar. But it's a big switch, and it will all take time.

A wind farm like this one promises clean energy for the future.

Pollution

There are all kinds of junk in the sea, from small cigarette butts to big containers that topple off ships. And plastic. Lots and lots of plastic. Humans use billions of plastic bags and plastic bottles that often get washed into the ocean. Plastic takes centuries to break down, so it piles up fast. Plastic is very bad for marine life. Birds, fish, and mammals sometimes mistake it for food and eat it, which over time is deadly.

Chemicals in the water can also make animals sick. Some poisonous substances build up in the bodies of fish. When larger mammals eat those fish, they get poisoned, too. It doesn't always kill them right away, but it makes them sick over time. Dolphins are some of the most toxic animals around, just because of what they eat. That condition makes it harder for them to fight off diseases.

Another pollution problem is oil. You may have heard that oil and water don't mix, and that's especially true in the ocean! When large oil spills happen in the ocean, it wreaks havoc on marine life. Oil is very irritating to the skin and fur of marine mammals. When they get covered in oil, their first instinct is to try to get it off. For many animals, that means licking their skin or fur to get clean, which makes them sick.

Underwater construction noise can damage wildlife.

Mammals with a lot of hair, such as sea otters, are especially at risk. Their hair covers a layer of air that keeps them warm. When they get covered in oil, it messes up their hair and destroys this layer of air. They can get **hypothermia** very quickly.

Sound Off

If you look around, you can see a lot of pollution. Now listen closely. Can you hear it, too? Imagine you are at a crowded party, trying to have a conversation with someone across the room. All the other people talking make it impossible.

Effects of sonar on marine mammals

That's the problem for marine mammals, too. They're surrounded by noise pollution.

People don't live in the ocean, but they're on it all the time, and they make quite a racket. The sounds and vibrations from ship engines carry through the water for long distances. Geologists use bursts of sound as a way to explore the bottom of the ocean, looking for natural resources like oil. The **sonar** blasts from a submarine can permanently damage the hearing of marine mammals. Even in the cases when the damage is not so severe, all that background noise drowns out what animals really need to hear—each other.

How bad is the problem? Some animals just seem to ignore the noise, or avoid it by going somewhere quieter, while others may start to get used to it. Some reports show that fishing boats in Alaska make a very specific sound. Sperm whales have learned to recognize it and actually approach the boats, hoping to find fish, leading to the risk of them getting tangled in fishing nets.

The Port of Boston is a busy place with ships constantly going in and out. Right whales often make their way into the port as well. To help prevent tragedies like what happened to Punctuation's calf, scientists have put out buoys with sensors that pick up whale calls. They can figure out where the whales are, and warn nearby ships to slow down and steer clear. It does not always work, but it helps.

In the 1990s, scientists from Cornell University began using "pop-ups." These devices float near the bottom of the ocean and record all the sound. After a few months, scientists pull them up and listen to what's going on— from whale calls to ship noise. It can help them determine where the noisiest places are and then figure out what to do about them. The National Oceanic and Atmospheric Administration (NOAA) is working on making a "sound map" of the ocean to show where the problems are.

Scientists are lobbying for stricter rules about where and when it's okay to

Coast Guard ships deploy buoys to track ocean noise.

make noise. For example, if a species uses a particular region to breed or give birth, the noise in that area should be reduced or stopped during the mating season. They are also working to get governments to cooperate with each other to agree to set limits on the total amount of noise.

There are some efforts to quiet things down altogether. For example, engineers can design ship propellers so they make a lot less noise. They can also soundproof rooms inside the ship so sound doesn't escape into the water.

 ## TEXT-DEPENDENT QUESTIONS

1. What is one problem facing California sea lions?
2. What is one way oil can hurt marine mammals?
3. What does a pop-up do?

 ## RESEARCH PROJECT

The oceans are polluted with plastic, and that's bad news for marine life. Find out more about how plastic is endangering animals, and what things are being done to help.

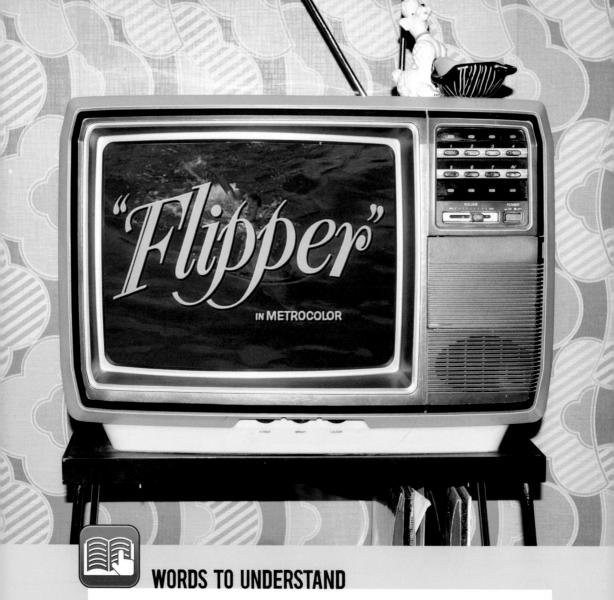

WORDS TO UNDERSTAND

forage to look for something, especially food

genetic having to do with an organism's genes; created and passed down by genes

habituate to become accustomed to something

sediment dirt, sand, and other material that settles at the bottom of a body of water

LOOKING TO THE FUTURE

To see a marine mammal in the 1960s, all you had to do was turn on the TV and watch *Flipper*, a popular show starring a friendly Florida dolphin. If you wanted to get up close and personal, there were marine animal parks opening up all over the country where trained dolphins and seals did tricks. Most of this gave people lopsided ideas of what marine mammals were really like. They were shown as friendly creatures happy to be at the service of humans, whereas in reality, they probably didn't want much to do with people. On the "flip" side, it did start to raise awareness of marine animals. People became more concerned with protecting them.

Growing Awareness

In 1972, the United States created the Marine Mammal Protection Act (MMPA). Under this new law, it was illegal to kill, capture, or interfere with any marine mammal. A year later, the Endangered Species Act was passed. Using this, the government worked to protect endangered animals and their habitats, creating a safety net for marine mammals.

Almost 50 years later, many marine biologists think the MMPA has worked, at least up to a point. Species like gray seals and sea lions have rebounded. One report showed that the population numbers of almost 20 percent of marine mammal species were improving, while only 5 percent were declining. What about the rest? Scientists don't know. Marine mammals are hard to study and track and we don't have enough data for most species. Some of them may need new forms of protection.

A key way to do this is to provide habitat. There are hundreds of protected marine areas across the world. All together, they still only represent about 3 percent of the world's oceans. Many of them are concentrated in coastal areas. This is a good start, because many marine mammals live near the coasts. However, there need to be more such areas, and they need to be bigger.

MAKE WAY FOR MANATEES

The Florida manatee does not like to be cold. When the water dips below 68 degrees, they cannot survive for long. In northern Florida, warm water comes up from the ground at many natural springs. These can make great places for manatees to hang out when the weather gets chilly.

The problem is, they can't reach them. **Sediment** has built up on the ground, and the water is too shallow for a 1,200-pound (544 kg) manatee. In 2010, the U.S. Fish and Wildlife Service joined with the environmental group called the Nature Conservancy to help the manatees. They cleared out Three Sisters Springs in Crystal River, Florida, to make it a few feet deeper. When cold weather moved in soon after, there were 200 manatees at Three Sisters enjoying a nice warm bath.

Beyond Borders

To effectively protect habitats, there will need to be cooperation between different nations. It won't be enough if just a few nations pledge to create protected areas and not dump trash in the ocean. If their next-door neighbors are doing those things, it will affect everyone.

There have been some efforts to encourage cooperation. In 1986, for example, 25 countries around the Caribbean came together at the Cartagena (Colombia) Convention. They agreed to work together to prevent oil spills in the

Australia's Great Barrier Reef is UNESCO-protected.

ocean. Later they also agreed to create protected marine areas, and stop land pollution from getting into the water.

One hurdle in identifying protected areas is figuring out who owns them in the first place. Almost every part of the Earth's land, with the notable exception of Antarctica, is owned by some country. The ocean is a different story. Countries usually control a couple of hundred miles of water out from their coastlines. Beyond that are the "high seas"—and nobody owns those.

The United Nations (UN) may be able to do something about that. The UN includes nearly every country in the world working together on international issues. An agency within the UN called UNESCO is dedicated to preserving certain places in the world—places that are scientifically or culturally important. However, the agency can only protect places that are part of a UN country and that puts most of the ocean out of its reach. In 2016, UNESCO named five places in the ocean that are also noteworthy. There are two in the Atlantic Ocean, two in the Pacific Ocean, and one in the Indian Ocean. They are all home to important ecosystems. UNESCO suggested that these places could also be recognized and preserved as important sites—if everyone agreed to it.

Studying Marine Mammals

Tagging dolphins.

Biologists know that marine mammals are a lot different from their cousins on land. Of course they live in different places and eat different things. Their bodies have evolved so they can live easily in or around water. Unfortunately, a lot of what we know comes from "stranding science." This is the study of dead or injured animals found on beaches or in shallow water. Some information comes from studying live animals held in captivity. Neither of these situations is ideal. However, studying marine mammals in their natural habitat is difficult since humans do not live in water.

Over the last few decades, scientists have come up with some creative ways to get more information. Putting tags on individual animals lets them track where and when animals travel. Electronic tags can send back data remotely so scientists can follow the animals in real time. The tags also provide information about the environment the animals are in—such as the depth and temperature of the water.

In some cases, it's possible to study marine mammals more directly. In 1970, when Randy Wells was in high school, he helped with a project to tag a pod of bottlenose dolphins. The dolphins were in Sarasota Bay, off the west coast of Florida in the Gulf of Mexico. Researchers wanted to find out if the dolphins lived there all the time, or if they were just traveling through. Now, almost 50 years later, Wells is the director of the Sarasota Bay Dolphin Research Program. It is the longest-running study of marine mammals anywhere in the world. Scientists have been studying some of the same dolphins for decades. They have learned a lot about the behavior and health of dolphins. They know more about how they communicate and what makes them sick. They also have a database of DNA samples to show what their **genetic** structure is like.

Scientists take DNA samples from sea lions.

Beggar got a lot of attention for his human-friendly ways.

Help from Humans

Beggar was one dolphin who lived in Sarasota Bay. He got his name because he liked to scavenge food from people. Sure, he ate fish, but he was just as likely to eat fishing hooks and lines. He might have a hot dog and chips for lunch (and a Twinkie for dessert). In 2012, Beggar was found dead. Biologists think his junk-food diet made him very unhealthy. Also, because he liked to approach humans to get food, he was much more likely to get hit by a boat.

Some animals are more naturally outgoing than others. That can be a problem when it comes to humans. The animals **habituate** to people, meaning they get used to being around them. Unfortunately, sometimes people want to cause them harm. Wild animals can't tell the difference between a person who wants to hurt them and someone who is just curious. Also, people can harm animals simply by petting or feeding them. If the animals start to depend on food from humans, they lose their ability to **forage** for themselves.

Still, when a marine mammal is seriously sick or injured, it's often humans who come to the rescue. Sometimes marine mammals get stuck when they strand themselves on a beach. They may be sick, injured, or lost. These animals are not built to live on land or even in shallow water. When an animal strands, it may have only a couple of hours to live if it does not get back in the water.

As part of the 1972 MMPA, a marine mammal stranding network was created. Rescuers in the network are ready 24/7 to come and help. They splash the animal to keep it cool while waiting for the equipment they need. It often takes nets, harnesses, cranes, and a lot of pushing and pulling by people to move large animals. If the animals are able to move, rescuers may play recordings of the animals' sounds to coax them back out to sea.

Sometimes the animals may not be able to survive if they are put back in the wild. Then, rescuers try to take them to a nearby shelter where veterinarians can help them.

A special hospital was opened in Hawaii for Hawaiian monk seals, with a kitchen to make seal food and pools for pups to play in. This critically endangered species has only about 1,000 animals left. The hospital helps the babies live long enough to be safely reintroduced in the wild.

Holding animals in captivity is a controversial issue. It can be a good solution for animals that are sick or hurt. They may not be able to survive in the wild. In other cases, certain animals are encouraged to breed. This can help endangered species in particular.

However, the case against captivity is strong. Opponents point out that living in captive places is unnatural and causes the animals a great deal of stress. They usually do not live as long as they would in the wild. Even when babies are reintroduced into the wild, they often do not have the skills to live on their own. They do not know how to search for food or protect themselves from predators.

Humans could not help the calf of Punctuation, the whale killed by a ship in 2016. A few months later there was good news: Punctuation herself had been sighted off the coast of Maine, alive and well. She might have another calf.

People usually think of trees and plants when they picture a healthy planet. But the oceans take up a lot more space than plants, and there's a lot more in them. To keep the whole Earth healthy, people need to "go blue" as well as "green." Saving marine mammals is about more than an individual animal or even a whole species.

It's about what happens to all of them put together.

TEXT-DEPENDENT QUESTIONS:

1. When was the Marine Mammal Protection Act created?
2. What kind of dolphins live in Sarasota Bay, Florida?
3. Name one way rescuers try to help stranded animals.

 RESEARCH PROJECT

Look into what researchers in Sarasota Bay, Florida, have discovered about the dolphins there. Design your own research project on dolphins. What would you want to find out? What things would you look for?

Pick an animal. Are you drawn to dolphins? Mad for manatees? Whatever marine mammal interests you, there is probably a group dedicated to helping it survive. Search the Internet to find one, and  read more about the animal's circumstances and what's being done to help. Many groups welcome volunteers, and for a donation you may be able to "adopt" an individual to help keep it safe.

Learn about your region. Check out the website for the National Oceanic and Atmospheric Administration (NOAA). This agency works throughout the United States to restore habitats in coastal areas, rivers, and wetlands. There's also information on how marine mammals in the U.S. are being helped by this work.

Look for volunteer opportunities. There are hundreds of groups dedicated to saving wildlife, including marine mammals. If you live in a coastal area, you may be able to join volunteer efforts for rescuing stranded animals or tagging them for research. One place to start is the Marine Mammal Center, which has several locations in California and one in Hawaii. Other local and regional groups are located throughout coastal regions in the U.S. Check out what's out there!

Consider your career options. Marine mammal science is always growing. It's more difficult to study marine mammals than land ones, so what scientists find out is important to understanding the biology and behavior of marine mammals. It's also possible to become a veterinarian specializing in caring for marine

mammals. There aren't many out there. After going to school to become a veterinarian, most marine vets take internships at marine mammal centers and learn more on the job.

Help the oceans. With oceans covering 70 percent of the world's surface, it's vital to keep them healthy. Organizations like the Ocean Conservancy and Oceana are working on various issues, such as cutting back on pollution, cleaning up trash, reintroducing habitats, and preventing overfishing.

FIND OUT MORE

BOOKS:

Fichter, George. **Whales, Dolphins, and Other Marine Mammals**. New York: St. Martin's Press, 2001.

Furstinger, Nancy. **12 Marine Animals Back from the Brink**. Mankato, MN: Riverstream Publishing, 2015.

Macquitty, Miranda. **DK Eyewitness Books: Ocean**. New York: DK, 2014.

Stefoff, Rebecca. **Sea Mammals**. New York: Cavendish Square Publishing, 2008.

Turner, Pamela S. **The Dolphins of Shark Bay**. New York: HMH Books for Young Readers, 2013.

WEBSITES:

kids.nceas.ucsb.edu/mmp/
Watch videos of dolphins swimming, listen to whale sounds, and learn about all kinds of different marine mammals here.

www.marinemammalcenter.org/
Check out the projects going on at the Marine Mammal Center in California.

www.education.noaa.gov/Marine_Life/Marine_Mammals.html
Play games, read up on different species, and learn about scientists' work at the National Oceanic and Atmospheric Administration.

SERIES GLOSSARY OF KEY TERMS

acidification the process of making something have a higher acid concentration, a process happening now to world oceans

activist someone who works for a particular cause or issue

biodiverse having a large variety of plants and animals in a particular area

ecosystem the places where many species live, and how they interact with each other and their environment

habitat the type of area a particular type of animal typically lives in, with a common landscape, climate, and food sources

keystone a part of a system that everything else depends on

poaching illegally killing protected or privately-owned animals

pollination the process of fertilizing plants, often accomplished by transferring pollen from plant to plant

sustain to keep up something over a long period of time

toxin a poison

INDEX

PHOTO CREDITS

Dreamstime.com: Simonegroup 10, Ekays 12, Wolgin 14, Imagezebra 15, Dhpropphotog 17, Melissaf84 18, Carole Cross 22, Tossi66 24, Andreas Alternburg 30, Paula Fisher 31, Twildlife 34, Vladislav Gajic 35, Tom Linster 38, Shao-Chun Wang 40, Flip Fuxa 41, Edmund Holt 42, Lucian Milasan 48, Greg Amptman 51, Arenacreative 56, Izanbar 60, Halim Hadi 61. Newscom/Kevin Dietsch/UPI 26; US Navy 44; US Coast Guard 46; Wikimedia: 29; NOAA: 6, 8, 21 (Dan Shapiro), 52 (Claire Fackler), 55.

ABOUT THE AUTHOR

Diane Bailey has written dozens of non-fiction books for kids and teens, on topics ranging from sports to science. She has two sons and lives in Kansas.

31192021550726